RECOGNIZE *Your* SIGNIFICANCE

52 Ways to See the Opportunity, Take Inspired Action and Live the Dream

To Our New Friends at Ffald y Brenin—

We recognize your significance in our lives and in the body of Christ.

Enjoy the Journey,

Rodney & Valerie Johnson

RECOGNIZE *Your* SIGNIFICANCE

52 Ways to See the Opportunity, Take Inspired Action and Live the Dream

BY
H. RODNEY JOHNSON

THE TRINSPIRATION™
COLLECTION

© 2012 Refreshing Productions, Inc.

A **TRINSPIRATION™** comes from the prefix *tri,* which means *three* and from the root word, *inspiration.*

Put them together and you have a **TRINSPIRATION™**.

A **TRINSPIRATION™** is a three-word phrase of inspiration and encouragement, which will propel you to where you were always meant to be in the first place.

My friend and bestselling author of *Life! By Design,* Tom Ferry says, *"My definition of inspiration is being imbued with the spirit to act. Motivation without inspiration doesn't last."*

A **TRINSPIRATION™** is a command that we give ourselves to remind us to "act."

Refreshing Books
A Division of Refreshing Productions, Inc.
21049 Devonshire Street
Chatsworth, CA 91311

©2012 H. Rodney Johnson

All rights reserved, including the right to reproduce this book or portions thereof in any form whatsoever. For information, contact: Refreshing Books Subsidiary Rights Department,
PO Box 4355, Chatsworth, CA 91313.

Scripture quotations are from the New International Version, New Living Translation, New King James Version, and the King James Version. Used by permission.

Quotes by Jim Rohn, American's Foremost Business Philosopher, reprinted with permission from Jim Rohn International ©2011.

TRINSPIRATION™ is a trademark of Refreshing Productions, Inc.

For information on booking H. Rodney Johnson to speak at your event, please call 818-882-5735.

ISBN: 978-0-9817708-0-2

RECOGNIZE YOUR SIGNIFICANCE

TABLE OF CONTENTS

INTRODUCTION	9
WEEK ONE: DARE TO DREAM	12
WEEK TWO: WRITE IT DOWN	14
WEEK THREE: CONTROL YOUR THOUGHTS, CONTROL YOUR WORLD	16
WEEK FOUR: FIND YOUR PASSION	18
WEEK FIVE: ASK POWERFUL QUESTIONS	20
WEEK SIX: IDENTIFY YOUR STRENGTHS	22
WEEK SEVEN: PLAN YOUR WORK	24
WEEK EIGHT: PHONE A FRIEND	26
WEEK NINE: COUNT THE COST	28
WEEK TEN: GET IN MOTION	30
WEEK ELEVEN: VISUALIZE THE OUTCOME	32
WEEK TWELVE: TRAIN YOUR MIND	34
WEEK THIRTEEN: DECLARE YOUR INTENTIONS	36
WEEK FOURTEEN: TRUST YOUR INSTINCTS	38
WEEK FIFTEEN: SEIZE THE DAY	40
WEEK SIXTEEN: SPARK THEIR INTEREST	42
WEEK SEVENTEEN: TAKE THE SHOT	44
WEEK EIGHTEEN: REV YOUR ENGINE	46
WEEK NINETEEN: EXCEED THEIR EXPECTATIONS	48
WEEK TWENTY: EXPECT THE BEST	50
WEEK TWENTY-ONE: ROTATE YOUR TIRES	52
WEEK TWENTY-TWO: EXAMINE YOUR ZIPPER	54
WEEK TWENTY-THREE: FOCUS YOUR ENERGIES	56
WEEK TWENTY-FOUR: PLANT A SEED	58
WEEK TWENTY-FIVE: REAP YOUR HARVEST	60

RECOGNIZE YOUR SIGNIFICANCE

Week Twenty-Six: **Live for Today**	62
Week Twenty-Seven: **Nod Your Head**	64
Week Twenty-Eight: **Laugh Out Loud**	66
Week Twenty-Nine: **Dance Like David**	68
Week Thirty: **Sing a Song**	70
Week Thirty-One: **Take a Hike**	72
Week Thirty-Two: **Choose Your Battles**	74
Week Thirty-Three: **Follow Your Heart**	76
Week Thirty-Four: **Stay the Course**	78
Week Thirty-Five: **Fire It Up**	80
Week Thirty-Six: **Soar With Eagles**	82
Week Thirty-Seven: **Push the Limits**	84
Week Thirty-Eight: **Turn It On**	86
Week Thirty-Nine: **Go the Distance**	88
Week Forty: **Play Your Game**	90
Week Forty-One: **Renew Your Strength**	92
Week Forty-Two: **Zip It Up**	94
Week Forty-Three: **Blast Your Past**	96
Week Forty-Four: **Wrestle an Angel**	98
Week Forty-Five: **Compete to Win**	100
Week Forty-Six: **Keep Short Accounts**	102
Week Forty-Seven: **Keep the Change**	104
Week Forty-Eight: **Unhinge the Gate**	106
Week Forty-Nine: **Discover Your Destiny**	108
Week Fifty: **Pay it Forward**	110
Week Fifty-One: **Testify to Love**	112
Week Fifty-Two: **Leave a Legacy**	114

INTRODUCTION

This book was originally slated to be titled *Take the Shot* because that was the first TRINSPIRATION™ phrase I ever used to encourage someone. At the time, I had yet to coin the term TRINSPIRATION™ because I hadn't realized the power of these three-word phrases to influence people for good. The back story is I was playing basketball on a church league when I kept noticing this guy from an opposing team who had a great shot. However, when he was open, he would usually pass off to someone else rather than taking the shot. Part of that was due to him having some real "hot dogs" on his team who were always asking for the ball. Maybe I should say, *demanding* he throw them the ball. Also, another reason he kept passing up open shots is he lacked confidence, even though he had a natural form. One day I saw him at church and I pulled him aside.

"I have three words to say to you, and I suspect they apply to more than just basketball. The three words are: *Take the Shot!*"

"You're right," he replied. "I do need to 'Take the Shot' in my life, my business and my family, as well as on the basketball court."

It wasn't until five years or more later that I even remembered this conversation. When another friend told me she had three words for our pastor, I remembered my earlier talk with this man. As a result

RECOGNIZE YOUR SIGNIFICANCE

of being reminded how I encouraged someone to *Take the Shot*, I began collecting three-word phrases. Over the course of several years, a pattern began to emerge. I noticed that the really impactful ones were imperative sentences in which the subject, "You," is understood. In other words, "You" *take the shot*. Or "You" *dare to dream*. Other phrases like "Find Your Passion," "Go the Distance," "Follow Your Heart," immediately came to mind and they, too, had "You" as the understood subject.

What I began to realize is phrases that stirred me were, in essence, mini-commands. There are times when I need to *Take the Shot*. There are other times when it would be easier to stop a project—like finishing this book—but then I give myself a command to *Go the Distance*.

As I began collecting these pithy aphorisms, I also saw they had the power to move people. When I began writing on my friends' Facebook walls on their birthdays the following:

A birthday TRINSPIRATION 4U:
"Recognize Your Significance"

I knew I had hit on something. The response was usually an immediate "Like" on my post. Moreover, I sensed that most people do not recognize their significance. When I encouraged them to recognize their significance, it did more than just provide a "warm fuzzy." It was a call to action: "Recognize Your Significance." You matter to me. You matter to more people than you realize. You have a calling that will affect those around you for good. But if you don't "Recognize Your Significance," you end up playing small and passing the ball off

RECOGNIZE YOUR SIGNIFICANCE

when you have an open shot. In fact, most people probably feel they are insignificant because of the billions of people alive on the earth. However, we all want to feel significant and feel that our life has meaning. I know I do and if you're honest, you feel the same way.

So, after consultation with two of the most "significant" people in my life—my wife and my coach—I decided to change the title from *Take the Shot* to *Recognize Your Significance*. If you begin to *Recognize Your Significance*, you will also start to *Take the Shot!* So let's get started on the road to significance.

RECOGNIZE YOUR SIGNIFICANCE

WEEK ONE

DARE to DREAM

Undoubtedly one of the most significant and inspiring speeches of the Twentieth Century was Martin Luther King, Jr.'s "I Have a Dream." Dreams inspire us to press on when society would hold us back. A dream will sustain us when all hope seems gone. Therefore, don't give up on your dream.

If life throws you a curve ball, dare to dream. If circumstances press in with excruciating cruelty, dare to dream. If it takes longer than you thought, dare to dream. The dream will die only if you give up.

Nurture the seeds of greatness within you and pull the dream-killing weeds out of the soil of your heart. You are destined to rule over the circumstances that would squelch your dream. Don't give up. Don't let it die. Dare to dream.

Live the Dream

The shame in life is not to fail to reach your dream, but to fail to have a dream to reach.
MOTIVATIONAL SPEAKER ROBERT J. KRIEGEL

Take Inspired Action

1. What is your dream? Write it down and post it in a place where you can see it every day.
2. Build a dream board to help you visualize your dream.
3. Create a time line and action plan for fulfilling it.

My Dream:

_____
_____
_____
_____
_____
_____
_____
_____
_____

Timeline and Action Plan for Fulfilling My Dream:

_____
_____
_____
_____
_____
_____

RECOGNIZE YOUR SIGNIFICANCE

Week Two

WRITE *It* DOWN

Lest you forget, write it down. Lest your vision lose its clarity, write it down. Lest you get to the end of a month, a year, or a life without accomplishing what you were destined to accomplish, write it down. Words have power, and when we can see those words, as well as hear ourselves speak them, faith begins to rise in our hearts. You are destined for significance. Dare to dream and then write it down.

Scientist, musicologist, and co-inventor of the Moog synthesizer, David Van Koevering, says that when we write something down, it amplifies our mind's capacity to retain the information by 700 times more than if we only hear it. Business coach, Glenn Dietzel says, "Writing is the doing part of thinking." I like that!

One of my life-changing examples of writing something down happened in December of 1981. As a 23-year old, I had moved to Los Angeles the previous January and was ready for a long-term relationship. Therefore, I wrote down that I wanted to meet a nice young lady. Within two months I met my wife and we were married the following December.

WRITE IT DOWN

LIVE THE DREAM

Write down the revelation and make it plain on tablets so that a herald may run with it.
An ancient prophet named Habakkuk

TAKE INSPIRED ACTION

1. Write down the five most important things to accomplish this week.
2. Carry it with you and check off the items as you complete them.
3. Write down your monthly goals, too.

My Top Five Priorities for the Week:

1. _____

2. _____

3. _____

4. _____

5. _____

Week Three

Control Your THOUGHTS Control Your WORLD

I had an epiphany recently as I stumbled across my bedroom in the dark at 5:22 am. I heard an inner voice say, "You can control your thoughts. And if you can control your thoughts, you can control your world." The first thing I noticed is that by controlling my thoughts I cannot control *the world* at large, but I can control my personal world. That "a-ha" moment of significance has transformed me in the last twelve days. My sales have gone through the roof.

Moreover, I've seen that the way I control my world is by controlling my actions. Our thoughts and actions are truly the only two things we can control. I refuse to participate in a recession or a depression. I challenge you today to take charge of your thoughts and actions and thereby control your world.

Live the Dream

If you do not take control of your inner thoughts, you will become a slave to your outer circumstances.
Dr. N. Cindy Trimm

Take Inspired Action

1. Decide to take control of your thoughts.
2. Identify the one area where you are weakest in controlling your thoughts and focus on overcoming the negatives by replacing them with positives.

Write down "the facts" of your most dominating negative thought. *(e.g. My body has a physical injury).*

_____
_____
_____
_____
_____
_____
_____

Now write down the "truth" about that negative thought. *(e.g. My body has healing powers residing within it that will cause me to walk in health and wholeness).*

_____
_____
_____
_____
_____
_____

RECOGNIZE YOUR SIGNIFICANCE

WEEK FOUR

FIND *Your* PASSION

If you are lacking clarity, this simple exercise will help you find your passion. Write down the ten things that really "get your juices flowing." For me, I wrote down selling luxury real estate, watching my kids play sports, being number one at something, creative writing, inspiring others to find and fulfill their passions, plus five others.

Then I took the first one on the list and compared it to the second one by asking myself, "Which one am I more passionate about?" Whichever one excited me most was put at the top spot. Then I compared the top thing to the third one on my list. If the third one stirred more emotions in me than my previous top choice, then it became my new number one. Then I would compare the new top choice to the second one on the list and so on down the line until I had achieved an order ranking from most passionate to least passionate.

Doing this exercise will provide clarity and clarity is what so many of us lack in our lives. If we have clarity about our passions, when an opportunity presents itself we will be able to respond appropriately by seeing where it fits on our "Passion Scale."

Find Your Passion

Live the Dream

Nothing great in the world has been accomplished without passion.
Georg Wilhelm

Take Inspired Action

1. Write down your top ten passions.
2. Rank them from most passionate to least passionate.

My Top 10 Passions:

1._____
2._____
3._____
4._____
5._____
6._____
7._____
8._____
9._____
10._____

RECOGNIZE YOUR SIGNIFICANCE

WEEK FIVE

ASK *Powerful* QUESTIONS

At the time of this writing, asking powerful questions has become one of the most important and significant things that I do. James, the brother of Jesus, said that we have not because we ask not. In short, we're either not asking for anything or we are asking the wrong questions for the wrong reasons. I remember asking God questions about life and then I would hear an inner dialogue in which my questions were answered by other questions.

One day I asked God, "Why do You always answer my questions with a question?" I heard, "Because the kingdom of heaven is within you and I want to draw it out of you." Talk about "significance." That was life-changing for me.

At the end of the first day of "Two-a-Days" her freshman year at college, my daughter Kelly called her mom and said that she didn't feel she had a very good touch on the soccer ball and her confidence level wasn't where she needed it to be. Valerie encouraged her to turn those assailing doubts into questions like "Why is my touch on the ball so strong?" She also suggested she ask, "Why am I playing with such strength and confidence?" At the end of the second day of practice the Associate Head Coach called her aside and said, "Now that's the Kelly Johnson we recruited. You were playing with real strength and confidence." So if you need wisdom, *Ask Powerful Questions.*

LIVE THE DREAM

*If any of you lacks wisdom, he should ask God,
who gives generously to all without finding fault,
and it will be given to him.*
JAMES, JESUS' BROTHER

TAKE INSPIRED ACTION

1. What is your most pressing issue for which you need wisdom? Write it down here: *(Example: I need to know how to make more sales so that I can pay off pressing debts.)*

2. Formulate a powerful question that will draw out the wisdom needed to resolve your pressing issue: *(Example: Why am I making more contacts, setting more appointments and having greater success than ever before?)*

RECOGNIZE YOUR SIGNIFICANCE

WEEK SIX

IDENTIFY *Your* STRENGTHS

High school and college counselors are known to give tests to their students to help them identify the areas where they are most likely to succeed based on their skills and aptitude. I remember a wood working teacher in high school giving us an aptitude test at the beginning of the semester. Being a silly teenager, I wrote that I am "apt to do" anything. However, if you want to succeed, you cannot be a jack of all trades, master of none.

A marketing consultant once asked my assistant who had known me for 15 years what she felt my strengths were. I was truly surprised by some of her answers. Sometimes we are blind to our own abilities. We see ourselves as one way while our supervisor, assistant, spouse, best friend, or teacher see something entirely different. Today, make a list of all of your perceived strengths. Then without telling the person what you wrote down, ask someone who knows you well to write down their opinion of your strengths. Then compare notes.

IDENTIFY YOUR STRENGTHS

LIVE THE DREAM

A true friend knows your weaknesses but shows you your strengths; feels your fears but fortifies your faith; sees your anxieties but frees your spirit; recognizes your disabilities but emphasizes your possibilities.
WILLIAM ARTHUR WARD

TAKE INSPIRED ACTION

1. Write down your top five strengths.
2. Ask someone who knows you well to do the same.
3. Compare your notes & start doing the things at which you are good and delegate the rest.

RECOGNIZE YOUR SIGNIFICANCE

WEEK SEVEN

PLAN *Your* WORK

Clichés abound around this TRINSPIRATION™. Undoubtedly you've heard at least one of them like "People don't plan to fail. They just fail to plan." Or "Plan Your Work and Work Your Plan." However, it is not a cliché that if you want to succeed, you need a plan. Every year in the fourth quarter, the business coaching organization I have been involved with helps their clients develop a plan for the following year. Whether you are a business person or a stay at home mom, everyone needs a plan.

My wife is the ultimate list maker. Even when she was staying at home while the kids were little, she had a plan for each day. That plan may have been to take the kids to the beach and have a fun day. Nevertheless, it was in writing. If you read the biographies of any successful business person, you will most likely hear about their written plans. Moreover, they had check points along the way to make sure they were on track. If you are following this book's weekly outline, you need to stop right now and make your plan. Whether it is for the day, the week, the month, the year or your career, put it in writing now.

PLAN YOUR WORK

LIVE THE DREAM

"For I know the plans I have for you," declares the LORD, "plans to prosper you and not to harm you, plans to give you hope and a future"
GOD

TAKE INSPIRED ACTION

1. Put your plan in writing.
2. Write down your top five or six priorities before beginning each day.

_____
_____
_____
_____
_____
_____
_____
_____

Week Eight

PHONE *a* FRIEND

When the game show, *Who Wants to Be a Millionaire*, took the nation by storm, many people began talking about the game's "Lifelines," particularly the one called "Phone a Friend." When John Carpenter became the first contestant to win the grand prize, he got to the last question without having used any of his "Lifelines," so he used his "Phone a Friend" to call one of the most significant people in his life—his father—to tell him he was going to win the million dollars.

By phoning a friend, you could be the "Lifeline" that someone needs. A listening ear could provide just the spark that will propel them to answer their own questions. Try this: call someone you have been meaning to reconnect with but haven't spoken to in ages. Your call will be a welcome surprise and could be just the thing that both of you need. Talk about making someone feel "significant."

PHONE A FRIEND

LIVE THE DREAM

Call unto Me and I will answer you, and show you great and mighty things which you do not know.
GOD

TAKE INSPIRED ACTION

1. Call the best man in your wedding or maid of honor.
2. Call your best friend from high school.
3. Call someone to whom you need to apologize.

Journal about your call here:

Week Nine

COUNT *the* COST

Buying fixer homes, repairing them, and then re-selling them can be lucrative. Going for a higher degree professionally can benefit your professional career. Training for a marathon will get you into great shape. What any significant achievement requires is a thorough assessment of the cost before initiating your plans.

If you don't know what the costs are, then ask someone who has done what you want to do how to calculate the cost. A person who has trained and run in an ironman triathalon can tell you firsthand about the cost in time and stress on your body. You may find that something really isn't that high of a priority once you realize the true cost. However, finding a worthy cause and paying the price will yield significant dividends.

COUNT THE COST

LIVE THE DREAM

"For which of you, intending to build a tower, does not sit down first and count the cost, whether he has enough to finish it—lest, after he has laid the foundation, and is not able to finish, all who see it begin to mock him, saying, 'This man began to build and was not able to finish.'"
JESUS

TAKE INSPIRED ACTION

1. Develop a detailed action plan, with associated costs, to achieve your goal.
2. Ask someone who is qualified to check your figures.
3. Proceed only after determining that the costs are something you are willing to pay.

My Plan:

_____
_____
_____
_____
_____

Costs and Projections:

_____
_____
_____
_____
_____

RECOGNIZE YOUR SIGNIFICANCE

WEEK TEN

GET *In* MOTION

Remember the law of inertia from elementary science class? Objects in motion tend to stay in motion and objects at rest tend to stay at rest. We've "Dared to Dream," "Written it Down," "Found Our Passion," and now it is time to "Get in Motion." Otherwise you will stay at rest and never do what you were destined to do. I am a firm believer that we are not here on planet earth by accident and that there is a divine purpose and significant calling on your life. However, you will never realize your destiny if you don't begin to take steps to achieve your destiny.

I have known people who say, "I'm just waiting on God." And they never do anything because they are still waiting. If you fall into that category, I'd like you to look at the word "waiting" in a different manner. Picture yourself as a waiter in a fine restaurant. If you want to earn large tips, you will "wait" on the customers by anticipating what they want next, refilling their water or drinks without having to be asked; you will be the most attentive waiter they have ever seen and your extra effort will not go unrewarded. Similarly, if you're waiting for your ship to come in, swim out to it. And speaking of ships, you can't turn a ship unless it is in motion. Likewise, if you want direction for your life, "Get in Motion."

Live the Dream

The least movement is of importance to all nature.
The entire ocean is affected by a pebble
Blaise Pascal

Take Inspired Action

1. Identify the first step to take to realize your goal.
2. Tell someone you trust what you are going to do and by what date you will have it completed.
3. Take that first step.

What is my first step?
___
___
___

What is my completion date & who did I tell?
___
___
___

RECOGNIZE YOUR SIGNIFICANCE

WEEK ELEVEN

VISUALIZE *the* OUTCOME

Before I started second grade, we moved to Peculiar, Missouri. That's right, *Peculiar,* MO. On the last day of school, we had an awards assembly and each teacher gave out different academic certificates. That is, everyone except the sixth grade teacher. Mr. Jay Cowan bought trophies for the top three students with the highest grade point averages. From second grade forward, my desire to receive the first place trophy once I reached sixth grade grew in intensity. In fact, on the last day of school when I was in fifth grade, I went up to Mr. Cowan and told him that next year, I was going to be his #1 student. I declared my intention. When school started in late August, I had already determined that I was going to work harder than any other student in the sixth grade. If Mrs. Orr assigned an English paper, I would include footnotes, even if she didn't require them. If Mr. Cowan had us create a book about preserving the environment, I took extra care with binding mine. Then each night before I went to sleep, I would see myself standing before the students on the last day of school and Mr. Cowan handing me the trophy for having the best grades. To reach your goal, visualize the outcome. Oh, by the way, I got the first place trophy.

VISUALIZE THE OUTCOME

LIVE THE DREAM

Then He brought him outside and said, "Look now toward heaven, and count the stars if you are able to number them." And He said to him, "So shall your descendants be."
GOD TO ABRAHAM

TAKE INSPIRED ACTION

1. Before you go to sleep, picture your desired outcome.
2. Create a dream book, putting in photos of your goals.
3. Take a three-minute break in the middle of the afternoon, close your eyes, and visualize the desired outcome for your next task.

Write out the name of your dream book here:

_____

WEEK TWELVE

TRAIN *Your* MIND

Did you know that you don't have to accept every thought that comes into your mind? Some people live in fear and shame that they are going to be found out as a horrible person because of a bad thought they entertained. Instead of dismissing the thought as soon as it comes in, they castigate themselves for even having the thought in the first place. You don't choose every thought that comes to your mind; however, you *do* choose whether you're going to keep thinking about it or not.

Our minds can and should be trained just like athletes train their bodies. If you don't have a plan for training your mind, your mind is not being renewed. Don't waste another day of neglecting your most precious asset—your mind. Like a Roman sentry escorting a person to prison, begin today to take captive every thought and escort the ones you don't want right out of your thought life.

Train Your Mind

Live the Dream

Do not conform any longer to the pattern of this world, but be transformed by the renewing of your mind.
The Apostle Paul

Take Inspired Action

1. Wear a rubber band around your wrist.
2. Pop it when a thought appears that you don't want.
3. Replace that negative thought with something positive.

Write down the thoughts that tend to make you think negatively here:

_____
_____
_____
_____
_____

Write down a different positive outcome from what you've written above:

_____
_____
_____
_____
_____

Week Thirteen

DECLARE *Your* INTENTIONS

I started a practice seven years ago that has served me well. Each morning, one of the first things I do is write down ten things for which I am grateful. Then I write down ten things that I want to receive into my life. Finally, I write down what my intentions are for that particular day. If I have an appointment to be in front of a seller who wants to sell or a buyer who wants to buy, I declare my intention of helping them to that end. If I'm going to my daughter's soccer game, I declare that I am going to enjoy the game.

Declaring your intentions is not an easy task. Just ask the young man who wanted to date one of my daughters. I asked him point blank what his intentions were toward her. However, that exercise helped him clarify a lot of points in his mind.

Declaring your intentions on a daily basis helps you to prioritize what is really important for that day. I challenge you to add this to your morning routine and see your world dramatically change over the ensuing weeks and months. To really turn up your results, ask God what His intentions are for you! Get ready for some mind-altering thoughts.

Declare Your Intentions

Live the Dream

Our intention creates our reality.
Dr. Wayne Dyer

Take Inspired Action

1. Write down your intentions every day.
2. Find someone you trust to share your intentions daily.

List ten things for which you are grateful:
1. _____ 2. _____
3. _____ 4. _____
5. _____ 6. _____
7. _____ 8. _____
9. _____ 10. _____

List ten things you want to receive into your life:
1. _____ 2. _____
3. _____ 4. _____
5. _____ 6. _____
7. _____ 8. _____
9. _____ 10. _____

Declare your intentions for today:

_____
_____
_____

Week Fourteen

TRUST *Your* INSTINCTS

I missed out on two large sales because I didn't trust my instincts. While driving north, I felt prompted to go by three new houses that had recently been built. As I turned around in the cul-de-sac, the owner of one house pulled into her driveway. Instead of stopping to introduce myself, I drove on. Later that week, she listed her house for $1.2 million. Then a few days later I had another prompting to call my friend, Chuck. Since I didn't have his number with me, I delayed and ultimately forgot to call him. Again, a few days later Chuck listed his house for sale and I missed out on the second sale. I learned my lesson, though. Now when I get that "impression" to call someone or drive through a certain area I do it. As a result of trusting my instincts, I called a man I had never met and he was ready to buy and sell. We did $2.5 million in business one summer because I acted on my instincts.

When you feel that "nudge" to call someone, do it. You may be the cause of a pattern interruption that keeps them from doing something irresponsible. When you have that "impression" to go home a different way, do it. You may avoid a major collision on the freeway by doing so. Had I made the call to Chuck and had I introduced myself to the homeowner, I could have potentially sold $1.7 million in real estate that week.

Live the Dream

Your ears shall hear a word behind you, saying, "This is the way, walk in it," whenever you turn to the right hand or whenever you turn to the left.
The Prophet Isaiah talking about God

Take Inspired Action

1. Pay attention to those impressions, nudges, hunches, instincts, and "inward witnesses" that prompt you to do something different or out of the ordinary.
2. Decide now to obey them when they come.
3. Keep a journal of what happens when you "trust your instincts" and tell others about the results.

_____
_____
_____
_____
_____
_____
_____
_____
_____

Week Fifteen

SEIZE the DAY

Carpe diem. The Latin phrase translated *seize the day* was brought to the public's attention with the movie *Dead Poets Society*. On his first day of teaching English literature at an East Coast boy's boarding school, Robin Williams gathered his young pupils around the trophy case and intoned the words *carpe diem*. His delivery had these adolescent boys yearning to believe that they could *suck the marrow out of life* and truly live a meaningful life.

He inspired them to find meaning in literature and poetry. We've all undoubtedly had a teacher, a coach or a mentor who has encouraged us to be more and do more. Reflect on what it was about that person who recognized your gift and caused you to believe that you could follow your dream. Someone once said that today is a gift. That's why it is called the present. Unwrap yours and seize the day.

SEIZE THE DAY

LIVE THE DREAM

Men make history, and not the other way around. In periods where there is no leadership, society stands still. Progress occurs when courageous, skillful leaders seize the opportunity to change things for the better.
HARRY S TRUMAN

The right man is the one who seizes the moment.
GOETHE

TAKE INSPIRED ACTION

1. Write a letter of thanks to a mentor or teacher.
2. Start each day with a plan to "seize the day."
3. Start from a place of gratitude and list 10 things for which you are grateful.

To whom will you write your letter of thanks?
_____

What are some things you want to say in your letter?
_____
_____
_____
_____
_____
_____
_____

RECOGNIZE YOUR SIGNIFICANCE

WEEK SIXTEEN

SPARK *Their* INTEREST

Whether we want to admit it or not, we are all in sales. You think not? Just try getting a date. In order to get that "sweet thing" to say, "Yes," you've got to get her interest. To get a promotion you must show the boss that you have leadership potential. In short, virtually everything we do involves the sales process. And the first rule of sales is to get your customer's attention.

Allowing negativity to come out of your mouth by saying things like, "I don't have any sales skills," will become a self-fulfilling prophecy. Instead, begin to allow your creativity to blossom forth and expect interesting ideas to come to you. Make it a habit to think different from others and you'll be surprised at the ways you can get the attention of the person who needs your service or product.

Live the Dream

All Fords are exactly alike, but no two men are just alike. Every new life is a new thing under the sun; there has never been anything just like it before, never will be again. A young man ought to get that idea about himself; he should look for the single spark of individuality that makes him different from other folks, and develop that for all he is worth. Society and schools may try to iron it out of him; their tendency is to put it all in the same mold, but I say don't let that spark be lost; it is your only real claim to importance.

Henry Ford

Take Inspired Action

1. Set aside times each week to think creatively.
2. Write down your best ideas and then refine them.
3. Put a note pad by your bed to write down ideas that come in the night. Better yet carry a note pad with you at all times or speak your ideas into a recording device on your phone.

What is your best thought today?

_____

_____

_____

RECOGNIZE YOUR SIGNIFICANCE

WEEK SEVENTEEN

TAKE *the* SHOT

UCLA's (University of California at Los Angeles) legendary basketball coach, John Wooden, used to design plays for his players that would allow them to "take the shot" in their favorite spots on the court. Intuitively, he knew that if they could get open where they liked to shoot, their chances of making a basket increased dramatically. Just like the athletes who brought home 11 national championships under Wooden's tenure, you also have skills and abilities at which you excel.

Today, take the initiative and do something that you know you are good at but never had the nerve to try. You'll need practice and scrimmages to get open for your chance to shine. In life, just as in the game of basketball, the one who wins is the one who will "take the shot." Be courageous. Go for a *three pointer!*

LIVE THE DREAM

You miss 100 percent of the shots you never take.
WAYNE GRETZKY

TAKE INSPIRED ACTION

1. Identify a dream you have neglected to pursue.
2. Make a list of the requirements to achieve this dream.
3. Like a basketball player shoots free throws, a golfer putts the golf ball, a soccer player takes shots on goal, practice role playing to get confident to "take the shot."

What is your neglected dream?
_____
_____
_____
_____
_____

What do you need to do to achieve that dream?
_____
_____
_____
_____
_____

Week Eighteen

REV *Your* ENGINE

For a middle-aged man, I drive a pretty hip truck. I didn't get it to draw attention to myself but it still has that effect nonetheless. I bought it used from a man who installed all sorts of after-market items on it that make it even more cool, including an air flow system that makes the engine not only perform better, but "sound" like it's *bad*. (For those of you still grappling with "less is more," *bad* equals *good* in this case). I used to walk in the mornings with a buddy and if he was standing outside waiting for me to arrive, he could hear my truck's engine as I came around the corner before I was in sight.

Sometimes people rev the engine of their car to keep it running if it has not been started in a long time. What are some items you have neglected to do that are crucial to your goals? If you don't do these things, the goal won't be reached. It will be like having a $100,000 car in your garage and never driving it. If you take action and "rev your engine," people will hear about you before they see you.

Live the Dream

Drive thy business or it will drive thee.
Benjamin Franklin

Take Inspired Action

1. Determine what actions or lack of action has kept you from your destiny.
2. Make a list of what has been neglected.
3. Whatever can be done today, do it.

Make a growl with your voice right now as if you are revving your engine. Come on now. You can do it.

Did you do it? If not, do it. I double-dog dare you to "Rev Your Engine."

Now make your list:

_____
_____
_____
_____
_____
_____

Week Nineteen

EXCEED *Their* EXPECTATIONS

Under promise and over deliver. By that I mean don't make promises that you cannot deliver within the agreed upon time frame. Have you ever noticed how amusement parks will post signs at the beginning of a long line for a popular ride stating that the estimated wait time is 45 minutes? When you arrive at the front of the line 30 minutes later, you are not angry about the wait. Actually, you may be pleasantly surprised that you "saved" 15 minutes.

What can you do for a client or a teacher that will exceed their expectations? When I wrote a term paper in sixth grade, I used college guidelines that went over and above the assignment. I received an A even though I had a couple of misspelled words. The teacher was obviously impressed by my exceeding her expectations.

EXCEED THEIR EXPECTATIONS

LIVE THE DREAM

The first step in exceeding your customer's expectations is to know those expectations.
ROY H. WILLIAMS

TAKE INSPIRED ACTION

1. Surprise your family or friends with a special activity.
2. Send a client an article that they will find helpful.
3. Give more than you were asked to give.

Who can you surprise with a special activity?
___

What will that activity be?
___
___
___

RECOGNIZE YOUR SIGNIFICANCE

Week Twenty

EXPECT *the* BEST

Years ago, a major national real estate franchise had the slogan, *Expect the best*. For awhile, I secretly wished that I worked for that company because they sold more million dollar homes than any other franchise. I wanted to move into that market, yet I wouldn't change from a company that had the expectation of selling mid-ranged houses. What I've learned is that the corporate leadership of both companies had a sense of expectation about market share that was imparted to its agents and the salespeople lived up to those self-fulfilling prophecies.

So why settle for mediocrity when the best is available? The best education, the best job and, ultimately the best life are yours for the taking. It all starts with a sense of expectation. If you don't expect to reach the best that life has to offer, the odds are exceptionally high that you won't attain it.

LIVE THE DREAM

Achievement is largely the product of steadily raising one's levels of aspiration and expectation.
JACK NICKLAUS

TAKE INSPIRED ACTION

1. Write down your three highest priority goals for this year.
2. Determine how these goals exemplify expecting the best.
3. Set them so high that they scare you.

Week Twenty-One

ROTATE *Your* TIRES

Every good mechanic knows that if you regularly rotate the back tires to the front and put the front tires on the back, you will significantly prolong the life of the tread. By rotating your tires, you will also have a much safer ride because the tires will be wearing more evenly. Analyzing your goals will undoubtedly reveal the need to do some "rotation."

Rotate out the negative influences in your life and replace them with positive ones. Rotate out the time-killers in your schedule and replace them with appointments that will take you one step closer to your goal. Delegate the easy tasks that someone else on your team can do and concentrate on doing the things that will make a significant difference. Now get going and rotate your tires.

Rotate Your Tires

Live the Dream

I've learned over the years that it doesn't matter where you pitch in the rotation. For me, preparation is everything.
Cory Lidle

Take Inspired Action

1. Determine where you are getting stuck in a rut.
2. Develop new actions to replace the ineffective one(s).
3. Give yourself 21 days to establish new habits.

What seems to be causing you to be stuck?
_____
_____
_____

What new actions will replace these ineffective ones?
_____
_____
_____
_____
_____
_____

RECOGNIZE YOUR SIGNIFICANCE

Week Twenty-Two

EXAMINE *Your* ZIPPER

Before you leave the house each morning, XYZ—examine your zipper. Before you stand to speak in public, XYZ. Before you leave the restroom, XYZ. To me, XYZ means more than just checking to make sure your pants are zipped. It's a reminder to check all of the small but important details in a project before it is turned in. Spell check on your computer won't tell you if you have used the wrong form of their/there, or poor/pour. You have to catch it yourself.

Publishers pay my company to proofread their authors' works before they are sent to the typesetter. It's another way to XYZ. Then they proofread it again after it has been typeset. If you go the extra mile and make sure you've done your homework properly, people who can further your career will appreciate the time you've spent "making your list and checking it twice." Furthermore, it also shows that you are diligent and reliable.

EXAMINE YOUR ZIPPER

LIVE THE DREAM

I tell you the truth, until heaven and earth disappear, not the smallest letter, not the least stroke of a pen, will by any means disappear from the Law until everything is accomplished.
JESUS CHRIST

TAKE INSPIRED ACTION

1. Ask a colleague to proof a project before turning it in.
2. Read your paper backwards to catch mistakes.
3. Check yourself in the mirror before leaving the house.

Always use spell check on your computer; however, read the paper and/or email backwards to check for errors, too.

Did you check yourself in the mirror before leaving the house? Good job!

Week Twenty-Three

Focus Your Energy

My daughter had a wake-up call after committing to play soccer for a Division 1 university. Her goals go beyond just playing at the college level. She has her sights set on playing on a national team. In talking with her club coach and her college coach, both told her that she has the potential to make a national team. Both of them have also told her about two areas that she needs to work on if she wants to fast-track herself onto achieving her goal. I tell her just like I'm telling you today, it is time to *Focus Your Energy*.

You have a destiny and, if you want to achieve it, you must eliminate the distractions that will keep you from it. For my daughter, it means less television time and more time practicing ball control. It means taking her workouts more seriously and giving up another athletic activity in order to make her soccer game her highest priority. You know what *you* need to focus on. In the words of Nike—*Just Do It*®.

FOCUS YOUR ENERGY

LIVE THE DREAM

Do you not know that in a race all the runners run, but only one gets the prize? Run in such a way as to get the prize.
THE APOSTLE PAUL

TAKE INSPIRED ACTION

1. Write down the one area that needs immediate focus.
2. Strategize how you can eliminate distractions.
3. Get started immediately.

Week Twenty-Four

PLANT a SEED

My life is a testimony to the truth you reap what you sow. And guess what? So is yours. As long as the earth remains, there will be seed time and harvest. We can count on that just as surely as we can count on the sun rising in the East and setting in the West.

Seeds are funny in that they produce after their own kind. In other words, you plant an apple seed—you get an apple tree. You plant a pumpkin seed and you get a pumpkin. We humans sometimes get it wrong. We plant seeds of gossip and are surprised when someone tells an untruth about us. We plant seeds of deceitfulness and are shocked when we are betrayed by the person we least expected to stab us in the back. I challenge you today to start sowing seeds of kindness, truthfulness, and generosity. Water them with love and nurture them as you would a rare tropical plant. Then harvest those seeds in season.

PLANT A SEED

LIVE THE DREAM

Now he who supplies seed to the sower and bread for food will also supply and increase your store of seed and will enlarge the harvest of your righteousness.
THE APOSTLE PAUL

TAKE INSPIRED ACTION

1. Give an anonymous donation to a worthy cause.
2. Write a letter to a teacher who helped you years ago.
3. Do a random act of kindness.

What is your favorite charity?
___

How much will you send them this week?
___

Who is that teacher who helped you?
___

What will you say in your letter?
___
___
___
___
___

RECOGNIZE YOUR SIGNIFICANCE

Week Twenty-Five

REAP *Your* HARVEST

Unless you are receiving a subsidy from the federal government not to plant a crop, every farmer I know plants with the intention of reaping a harvest. It is only logical. Not only does the farmer plant with the intention of harvesting, he watches over the plants during the "soil time" while the seed is receiving nourishment from the minerals in the ground and from the water.

My father-in-law calls "soil time" that period when the seed has been planted but there is no evidence that anything is happening. He says that if the seed could talk, it would say, "It sure is dark down here. I wonder if I'll ever see the light of day." Seeds have to die before they can grow into their destiny and ultimately be harvested.

Twenty-five years ago, I had to die to a dream in order for it to spring forth into a harvest of something totally new. If you are being called to lay down your dream, plant it as a seed and see a harvest reaped in a totally new area of your life. It happened for me and it can happen for you, too.

Live the Dream

What you give becomes an investment that will return to you multiplied at some point in the future.
Jim Rohn

Take Inspired Action

1. What part of your dream has died?
2. Plant that seemingly dead dream as a seed for a new harvest.
3. Keep your mouth closed if the harvest does not happen immediately; it may just be your seed's "soil time."

RECOGNIZE YOUR SIGNIFICANCE

WEEK TWENTY-SIX

LIVE *for* TODAY

As I stated earlier, as a kid, I could not wait for all of the milestone birthdays: being a teenager, turning 16 so I could drive, turning 18 so I could vote, etc. I was always looking ahead to the next "big" day. Now I love that saying that we are only given today—not tomorrow, not yesterday—and that's why it is called the *present*. If we begin to think of today as a *present* or *gift*, how will it affect what you do?

In his book, *The Five Love Languages,* author Dr. Gary Chapman says that we have one dominant love language. Mine is the receiving of gifts. If you want to show me that you love me, then give me a gift. On my fortieth birthday, my wife, Valerie, had a gift waiting for me at every place I stopped that day. When I came out of the gym, my car was filled with confetti and a small gift. When I got to the office, more gifts awaited my arrival. When I went to a meeting with a financial officer, believe it or not, there was a gift for me sitting on his chair. That Wednesday night at church there was gift number 40 waiting for me on the organ bench. So when you give me a gift, I know that you really think I'm special. How much more then should

LIVE FOR TODAY

I look at "today" as the gift that I have been desiring all of my life. If I do that, I truly will "live for today" and make the most of all that this day has to offer me.

Live the Dream

Learn from yesterday, live for today, hope for tomorrow.
The important thing is not to stop questioning.
ALBERT EINSTEIN

Take Inspired Action

1. Write down the best gift you have ever received.
2. Now write down the most important items that you need to accomplish today.
3. As you look over the items to accomplish today, view their completion as if you are being rewarded with your favorite gift.

What was the best gift you ever received?
_____
_____

What do you need to accomplish today?
_____
_____
_____
_____

RECOGNIZE YOUR SIGNIFICANCE

WEEK TWENTY-SEVEN

NOD *Your* HEAD

When the *Men in Black II* movie came out in the summer of 2002, its star, Will Smith, also had a hit rap song entitled *Nod Ya Head*. We nod our heads when music has an infectious beat like Smith's song. We nod our heads when we're tired and falling asleep, yet trying to stay awake. More importantly, we nod our heads when we are in agreement with something that is being said or done. Remember the obnoxious kid in high school who tried to brown nose the teacher? He was always nodding his head to show he agreed with her.

When two people agree, their power increases exponentially. It's not just a doubling. Today, you need to come into agreement about certain things. I encourage you to come into agreement over the truth. When you do this, it is liberating because the truth sets you free. Therefore, come into agreement, *Nod Ya Head,* and see the power released into your situation.

Live the Dream

"Again I say to you that if two of you agree on earth concerning anything that they ask, it will be done for them by My Father in heaven."
Jesus

Take Inspired Action

1. Write down the top two to three concerns you have that need agreement from other people in order to see the issue resolved.
2. Go to a like-minded person and ask for their agreement on the issue to be resolved.
3. Set a time with that person to discuss how it is being resolved.

What do I need agreement with from another person?
_____
_____
_____

Who is a like-minded person with whom I can share my concerns?
_____
_____

RECOGNIZE YOUR SIGNIFICANCE

WEEK TWENTY-EIGHT

LAUGH *Out* LOUD

With the advent of internet chat rooms where people from all around the world can converse without having to pay for long distance calls, there has sprung up a whole lexicon of abbreviations to expedite the "chatting." Probably the most famous abbreviation is LOL, which means to "Laugh Out Loud." Chatters type in this abbreviation when someone else online says something humorous or sarcastic.

Laughing out loud is very therapeutic. In fact, my wife used to regularly attend a Friday luncheon with her girlfriends that they dubbed the *Good Medicine Club.* This group got its name from the proverb that says a cheerful heart is good medicine. Their sole intent was to eat, play games and laugh. What they found was that laughing really did make them feel better. They looked forward all week long to getting together on Friday, eating some new dish that one of them had cooked, and then laughing while they played a new game.

LIVE THE DREAM

*A cheerful heart is good medicine,
but a crushed spirit dries up the bones.*
KING SOLOMON

TAKE INSPIRED ACTION

1. Rent a classic comedy and watch it tonight.
2. Call a friend who loves to tell jokes.
3. OK, open that friend's email who is always passing on jokes and have a good laugh.

RECOGNIZE YOUR SIGNIFICANCE

WEEK TWENTY-NINE

DANCE *Like* DAVID

Dancing with the Stars is one of the breakout reality shows of recent years. Professional ballroom dancers are paired with athletes, actors, singers, models, and activists not known for their dancing abilities. Heather Mills, an animal rights activist with a prosthetic leg, was featured in the 2007 season. Entertainment bloggers suggested people may have watched, out of morbid curiosity, to see if her leg would come off while she was dancing. Personally, I admired her willingness to take a risk.

Israel's most famous king had a serious fight with his wife, Michal, when she criticized him for passionately dancing before God as the Ark of the Covenant was brought back into Jerusalem. David was more concerned with honoring God than he was about the opinions of others. If you are going to make a mark in this world, you must pursue your dream passionately without being influenced negatively by those who don't share your vision. Like Heather and David, dance with all of your might and don't be concerned with what others think.

Live the Dream

*And David danced before the LORD
with all his might...*

Take Inspired Action

1. Put on some music and start moving.
2. Put passion into your work by acting enthusiastic.
3. Sign up for a dance class.

RECOGNIZE YOUR SIGNIFICANCE

WEEK THIRTY

SING *a* SONG

Guideposts editor, Rick Hamlin, shepherded an article for his magazine that was culled from the first chapter of my book, *Possessing Your Promised Land*. For Rick's fiftieth birthday, he decided to rent a hall, invite his friends, and do a concert of songs that he loved to sing. The pièce de résistance was when his two teenaged boys surprised him by showing up and performing the Beatles' "When I'm 64."

Whether it was Lennon and McCartney or Bach, Beethoven, and Brahms, music has provided the soundtrack to your life. The Bible records that the morning stars sang as creation was happening. In fact, everything in the universe is frequency and vibration. Your DNA is vibrating right now with a song that is uniquely yours. Only you can sing the song that is imprinted on your genes. Here's a piece of free advice: don't wait until you're 50 to start singing.

Sing a Song

Live the Dream

Sing to him a new song; play skillfully, and shout for joy.
King David

Take Inspired Action

1. Turn off talk radio.
2. Sing a happy song on the way to work.
3. Make up your own song and sing it with gusto.

Write the lyrics to your new song here:

_____
_____
_____
_____
_____
_____
_____
_____
_____
_____
_____
_____
_____
_____
_____

Email: *info@trinspiration.com* to be alerted to our upcoming TRINSPIRATION™ songs available on iTunes.

RECOGNIZE YOUR SIGNIFICANCE

Week Thirty-One

Take a Hike

We often hear the phrase, "Take a hike," used sarcastically by someone who doesn't want to be around another person. In his poem, "The Road Not Taken," Robert Frost writes, "*Two roads diverged in a wood, and I—I took the one less traveled by, and that has made all the difference.*" Let's look at taking a hike in a new light. Today, take a hike from sarcasm. Instead of saying something derogatory, choose the road less traveled. Take a hike from criticism. Require of yourself to say something positive about a person or a situation when your normal "path" would have been to criticize. Take a hike from apathy. That roadway is filled with people who could care less. Yet, something deep within you wants to care. Turn aside to the walkway of love and compassion. Take a hike from expecting the worst. Good things come to those who expect the best, not the worst. Everyone has at least one area in which they need to "take a hike." You are no different. Take a hike from complacency, get your boots on and start hiking.

TAKE A HIKE

LIVE THE DREAM

"Enter through the narrow gate. For wide is the gate and broad is the road that leads to destruction, and many enter through it. But small is the gate and narrow the road that leads to life, and only a few find it."
JESUS

TAKE INSPIRED ACTION

1. Pay someone a sincere compliment.
2. Change your expectations from the worst to the best by requiring yourself to find something positive about the person or the situation.
3. Literally "take a hike" to clear your mind and focus on something new.

Where will you go on your nature hike?

RECOGNIZE YOUR SIGNIFICANCE

Week Thirty-Two

CHOOSE *Your* BATTLES

I remember complaining to a friend about something that I didn't feel was right and I expected him to go to his superior to right the wrong. He said to me, "Buddy, you've got to choose your battles." He obviously did not think that my issue merited his involvement because he saw the bigger picture and my issue was just a minor skirmish in the whole scheme of things. Had he taken up my cause it could have burned up capital and credibility for things that truly mattered down the line. Even now as I write this, I don't have a clue what I wanted him to do. It obviously wasn't *that* important or I would have done something myself.

There are battles that are worthy of a fight. Civil rights, protection of family and friends, integrity, and truth immediately come to mind. I caution you about being goaded into a battle by someone who is out looking for a fight. As a freshman in high school, I was challenged to a fight by an upperclassman. Instead of engaging, I walked away. I was ridiculed for a long time after that, but I knew I had kept my integrity and my walking away landed a much harder blow to that young man's ego than any right hook I might have thrown.

Live the Dream

For we wrestle not against flesh and blood...
The Apostle Paul

Take Inspired Action

1. Analyze what is truly worth fighting for in your life.
2. Discuss with a good friend what is the best strategy for resolving the conflict at hand.
3. Recognize that the source of the battle most likely has a strong spiritual root in the other person's life.

What is the conflict?
___
___
___

RECOGNIZE YOUR SIGNIFICANCE

Week Thirty-Three

Follow Your Heart

My wife and I have the privilege of being the parents of three elite athletes. One pitched at the junior college level, one played NCAA Division 1 volleyball, and the youngest plays Division 1 soccer. As parents, one of the things we have attempted to do is to help our children find what they have a passion for and direct them toward excelling in that endeavor. They have explored other things such as piano, guitar, modeling, football, and softball but, ultimately, their hearts led them to their respective sports.

I'm in my fifties now and it is time to "follow my heart." No more procrastination. That is why you are reading this TRINSPIRA-TION™ right now. My desire is to encourage you to take action and see your dreams realized. That's why we are helping our children "follow their hearts," too. It's never too late. Get started on the process today and "Follow Your Heart."

Live the Dream

Whatever you do, work at it with all your heart...
THE APOSTLE PAUL

Take Inspired Action

1. Make that long postponed phone call, take a class, or join a club.
2. It's never too late to start living your dream.
3. Do whatever it will take to "follow your heart."

Who will you call?
_____

What class would you like to take?
_____

What club could you join?
_____

RECOGNIZE YOUR SIGNIFICANCE

Week Thirty-Four

STAY *the* COURSE

This TRINSPIRATION™ has been used by both Democrats and Republicans in the 20th Century. Lyndon B. Johnson used it in a speech about the Viet Nam war in 1967 and Ronald Reagan used it while campaigning for Republicans during the 1982 mid-term elections, encouraging the electorate to keep the country going on the same economic course he had started in 1980. No matter what party you belong to, once you commit to a project you should see it through to conclusion. Reagan did so on the economic front while our government did not commit to victory in Viet Nam. Both decisions have had far reaching impacts that have followed us into the 21st century.

Maybe you're thinking that your actions will not affect the world like a President's would. I guarantee that you are impacting the world of those who are in your sphere of influence. For me, just finishing this book demonstrates to my children the power of persistence. You've got a job to do and a course to finish. Don't let the winds of change pull you in a direction not of your choosing.

LIVE THE DREAM

I have fought a good fight, I have finished my course, I have kept the faith: Henceforth there is laid up for me a crown of righteousness, which the Lord, the righteous judge, shall give me at that day: and not to me only, but unto all them also that love his appearing.
THE MAN WHO WROTE TWO-THIRDS OF THE NEW TESTAMENT

TAKE INSPIRED ACTION

1. Make a list of the things most likely to divert you from your course.
2. Write down steps to take that will keep you focused on the task at hand.
3. Break them down into incremental steps that will keep you moving forward.

_____
_____
_____
_____
_____
_____
_____
_____

Week Thirty-Five

FIRE IT UP

Ask any elite athlete how to get to the next level and they will tell you to increase the intensity of your training. If you're in sales that means practicing your presentation daily until you know it backwards and forwards. If you're a writer, that means setting a schedule for writing and sticking to it no matter what. When you want to "fire it up," come to a project with a plan of focus and intensity.

You know the old joke of the person visiting New York who asked a native, "How do I get to Carnegie Hall?" The native replied, "Practice, man, practice." To achieve excellence in any field requires practice. There will be certain times when you will need to increase your intensity in order to go to the next level. Revel in those times. Pay the price of intense practice and then reap the rewards when you "fire it up."

FIRE IT UP

LIVE THE DREAM

*We went through fire and water,
but you brought us to a place of abundance.*
A PSALMIST

TAKE INSPIRED ACTION

1. Determine how you can increase your intensity to achieve your goal.
2. Outline a plan of focused intensity in your routine.
3. Execute the plan, keeping the goal in mind at all times.

What are the top two things you can do to increase your intensity? Write them here:

_____
_____
_____
_____

Outline for focused intensity:

_____
_____
_____
_____
_____
_____
_____
_____
_____

RECOGNIZE YOUR SIGNIFICANCE

Week Thirty-Six

SOAR *With* EAGLES

Eagles are not like turkeys—they don't flock together; they fly by themselves high above the turbulence. In fact, when the winds come, eagles will rise even higher above the storm. When a mother eagle is teaching her baby to fly, she will push it out of its nest and let it start falling on its own. Before the eaglet crashes to its death, she will swoop underneath with wings outstretched and provide a safe landing for her young.

In order for you to rise above your circumstances, you need to behave like an eagle. Going with the crowd, doing things the same way they've always been done will keep you in a rut. Find a quiet place, away from the crowd. Take time to listen to that still, small voice within so that you can rise above the distractions and soar with eagles. Then once you have your direction, step out of the nest. You are destined to soar.

Live the Dream

But they that wait upon the LORD shall renew their strength; they shall mount up with wings as eagles; they shall run, and not be weary; and they shall walk, and not faint.
A Prophet named Isaiah

Take Inspired Action

1. Make a list of what specific things are holding you back from soaring.
2. Find a quiet place and listen for direction.
3. Step out of your comfort zone and soar.

RECOGNIZE YOUR SIGNIFICANCE

Week Thirty-Seven

PUSH *the* LIMITS

Science tells us that the universe is ever expanding. Every day it grows more vast than the mind can even conceive. So, if our cosmos is programmed to keep growing exponentially, it stands to reason that we are the same way. I'm not talking about your girth but about your mental capacity. We have only just begun to scratch the surface as far as what mankind is capable of conceiving and achieving.

You haven't even begun to reach the limits of what you can do. Your brain is smarter than the world's largest computer, yet scientists tell us that even the most intelligent humans are using barely ten percent of their mental capacity. Turn off the television. Begin to study the things that are interesting to you. Even if you have Olympic medals on your mantle, you still haven't scratched the surface of your potential. So get ready, get set, and go *"push the limits."*

Live the Dream

*I'm competitive with myself.
I always try to push past my own borders.*
Tyra Banks

Take Inspired Action

1. Set aside 15-30 minutes each day to just think about what you love or what you want out of life.
2. Read a good book that challenges your old ways of thinking.
3. Study the life of Albert Einstein.

RECOGNIZE YOUR SIGNIFICANCE

Week Thirty-Eight

Turn It On

Every once in awhile, we need to crank up the volume—and not necessarily on our stereo. It's too easy to get complacent and stuck in a rut. If you've ever had your car stuck in the mud, you know that you have to put the "pedal to the metal" in order to move forward. Sometimes we need to be the one encouraging others to step onto center stage and do something really "out there." Life is too short to play it safe. We were created with passion and creativity, so quit censoring yourself and begin to live your life to its fullest potential.

Today, you have the opportunity to do something totally unique and different from anything you have done before. There will never be another time like today to take a new chance to break out of the old habits and try something new and exciting; therefore, *Turn it On!!!*

LIVE THE DREAM

Are you up to the challenge? Are you going to be a reproduction or an original? Will you strive to be innovative or imitative? Are you ready to take your turn on the page, turn up the heat, turn it on?
PHIL COUSINEAU

TAKE INSPIRED ACTION

1. Play some music really loud.
2. Pretend you are a contestant on *So You Think You Can Dance* and "Dance for your life" for the next 30 seconds.
3. Remove "I can't" from your vocabulary.

RECOGNIZE YOUR SIGNIFICANCE

Week Thirty-Nine

GO *the* DISTANCE

One of our family's favorite pastimes is watching the Olympics. We love both the winter and summer games. When our girls were young, they careened around the living room doing cartwheels after watching the gymnasts. However, being inspired by an Olympic athlete's stellar performance does not mean you can run out and join the team tomorrow. It takes a commitment of the highest order to make it to that pinnacle of success.

Realizing your goal starts with doing the small, intermediate steps now that will ultimately take you to your destination. Whether you are an athlete or not, to achieve your goal will require a plan and a coach to keep you going when you feel like quitting. Get started today and, by the way, enjoy the journey as you "go the distance."

GO THE DISTANCE

LIVE THE DREAM

It's not that I am so smart...
It's just that I stay with problems longer.
ALBERT EINSTEIN

TAKE INSPIRED ACTION

1. Recruit an accountability partner to keep you focused.
2. Celebrate each incremental success.
3. Read a biography of someone who went the distance.

Who will you ask to help you stay focused?

_____

What biography will you read in the next 30 days?

_____

RECOGNIZE YOUR SIGNIFICANCE

Week Forty

PLAY *Your* GAME

My nephew's high school basketball team had a new coach and was in a rebuilding season. The previous year this undisciplined team had been allowed to "run and gun" and play a type of "street ball" to less than stellar results. Therefore, the new coach had strict guidelines about how he wanted them to slow their game down and set up each play, instead of allowing certain players to "hotdog" and "grandstand;" it worked, too. Going into the district playoffs they were expected to place no higher than third. By playing their game, they beat the second seeded team in the semi-finals and blew out the first place team by 25 points in the finals.

Today, *Play Your Game* in the contest of life. If you don't know what to do yet, ask for wisdom and then move out once you've got the game plan.

PLAY YOUR GAME

Live the Dream

If there is a secret to success, it just might be little things done well.
JOHN WOODEN

Take Inspired Action

1. Ask for wisdom and expect to receive it.
2. Write out your game plan.
3. Proceed with confidence and determination.

RECOGNIZE YOUR SIGNIFICANCE

Week Forty-One

RENEW *Your* STRENGTH

Burn out happens when we don't take time to rest. Even God took a day off after creating the world. We would do well to follow His example. Sunday afternoon naps have become a staple in my repertoire for renewing my strength. Some people take "power naps" for 15-30 minutes and wake up refreshed.

Today, I called my son & told him that I was going to take photos of a house he was supposed to shoot just because I needed to get out of the office for awhile. Getting away for an hour left me feeling better about coming back and finishing my duties.

Scheduling time for doing something different and relaxing will make you more productive. Then you can approach a problem from a new perspective. Sometimes I will take a walk to the post office to clear my head. My wife and I look forward to walks through our neighborhood to catch up on what is happening in our work, our kids' lives, and our finances. Whatever relaxes you, make time for it on a weekly basis.

Live the Dream

Thus the heavens and the earth were completed in all their vast array. By the seventh day God had finished the work he had been doing; so on the seventh day he rested from all his work. Then God blessed the seventh day and made it holy, because on it he rested from all the work of creating that he had done.
God

Take Inspired Action

1. Take a power nap.
2. Take a walk through your neighborhood.
3. Do something relaxing.

Go call your favorite masseuse and schedule a massage!

RECOGNIZE YOUR SIGNIFICANCE

Week Forty-Two

ZIP IT UP

Did your mother ever tell you to "zip it up" because you were talking too much? It has happened to most of us. Too frequently, the more we open our mouths to justify our position or make an excuse, our "superfluity of verbosity" only makes it worse.

At our house, helping the kids get ready for school involves making sandwiches and getting other food that requires temporary storage in a zip-lock type of plastic bag. One manufacturer of such a product advertises that their bag "locks in freshness." When we learn to keep quiet, even though everything within us is screaming to speak our mind, we're like that plastic zip-lock bag—we bring a freshness to the atmosphere through our silence. An ancient king once said that even a fool is perceived as being wise when he keeps quiet.

Live the Dream

There is a time for everything...
a time to be silent and a time to speak.
King Solomon

Take Inspired Action

1. Think before you speak.
2. If it has already been said, keep quiet.
3. Ask yourself if your words will build up the hearer before you speak.

WEEK FORTY-THREE

BLAST *Your* PAST

In my days as a teenager, it was not uncommon to hear a disc jockey say, "Here's a blast from the past" followed by an oldie but goodie from, say, the '50s. Sometimes I will call someone I haven't spoken to in years and will start off the conversation with, "Paul, this is a blast from your past…Rodney Johnson." In both of these examples, the blast from the past is usually positive. However, the people closest to us tend to hold the past over us, particularly when we want to do something big, bold and new. You'll hear things like, "You could never do that because you don't have the education." Or you might hear, "You can't run that marathon, you have asthma." Unfortunately, those closest to us tend to see the limitations rather than the possibilities.

By saying, "Blast Your Past," I am not advocating telling anyone off or getting into an argument. What I intend is to prove them wrong. In college I took acting classes. One day an executive from a local advertising agency came to campus to audition people for commercials for a local bank. The acting teacher told certain people in the class to be sure to audition. He didn't tell me, though. He saw my limitations, so I set out to prove him wrong. I went to the audition and won the part. The commercial was so successful that the bank did a second one with me. I guess "blast your past" could be paired with "prove them wrong." And when you do succeed, have the self-discipline not to gloat. Your detractors will see the error of their ways. And if they don't, it's all right anyway. You will have made your point.

Live the Dream

We should not look back unless it is to derive useful lessons from past errors, and for the purpose of profiting by dearly bought experience.
George Washington

Take Inspired Action

1. What past failures have kept you from stepping out into your dream? Write them down.
2. What negative self talk has held you back? Write down a *positive* affirmation to "blast your past."
3. Begin the process of moving toward your dream by circumventing the negatives and holding a picture of the positive outcome you desire in your mind.

What positive affirmation will "reverse the curse" & "blast your past?" Write it here:

_____
_____
_____

RECOGNIZE YOUR SIGNIFICANCE

WEEK FORTY-FOUR

WRESTLE *an* ANGEL

There's a story in the Bible of a man named Jacob who was visited by an angel. They began to wrestle, and their wrestling match lasted all night long. Jacob wouldn't give up even when the angel touched his thigh and caused him to pull a muscle. Jacob said, "I won't let you go until you bless me." By the way, the angel did bless him and Joseph's twelve sons became heads of the twelve tribes of Israel. I guess Jacob intuitively knew that he was going to need help beyond his own means if he was going to fulfill the call on his life.

What is the call on your life? What help do you need to fulfill that call? Do you have the determination to hold on as long as it takes in order to fulfill that call? Who is your "angel" that has the key to unlocking the next door for you to move through? Answering these questions is part of the "wrestling" you need to do in order to prove you have got the power to stay in the match.

Wrestle an Angel

Live the Dream

And Jacob was left alone; and there he wrestled a man with him until the break of day. And when he saw that he could not prevail against him, he touched the hollow of his thigh; and the hollow of Jacob's thigh was out of joint as he wrestled with him. And he said, Let me go, for the day breaks. And Jacob said I will not let you go until you bless me. And the angel said to him What is your name? And he said Jacob. And the angel said Your name shall be no more called Jacob but Israel for as a prince you have power with God and with men, and you have prevailed.
GENESIS 32: 24-28

Take Inspired Action

1. Answer the four questions below.
2. Set an appointment with your "angel" (a mentor, a counselor) to discuss your dream/vision.
3. Ask three people who know you well to evaluate your strengths and point out areas of potential weakness.

What is the call on my life?
_____
_____

What help do I need to fulfill that call?
_____
_____

Do I have power to stay the course?
_____

Who is my "angel" with the key to the next door?
_____

RECOGNIZE YOUR SIGNIFICANCE

Week Forty-Five

COMPETE to WIN

All three of my kids love sports and love to compete. Put my son in to pitch with bases loaded, no outs and the winning runner at bat. Most of the time, he would get his high school baseball team successfully out of that situation. He thrives on competition. But he did not develop that mentality by playing on teams where we did not keep score. I don't think that philosophy helps children at all. Everyone needs to learn how to win graciously and lose without falling apart. Some of our best competitions come from competing against ourselves. For instance, in real estate I may try to list eight properties this month if I listed seven the previous month. Other times, I can challenge someone who is better than me in order to "up my game." One time I challenged a broker in New York City to see who could list the highest priced property before we were going to see each other at a real estate seminar in Las Vegas; we bet $100. I immediately listed a large house for $2.25 million. She bested me by listing one for almost $10 million. I learned from that experience that I can sell properties over $2 million in less than 30 days even if it did cost me $100 in our little bet.

Compete to Win

Live the Dream

The healthiest competition occurs when average people win by putting above average effort.
Colin Powell

Take Inspired Action

1. Write down your accomplishments from last month.
2. Write down how you want to exceed those accomplishments this month.
3. Challenge someone who is better than you to a friendly competition.

RECOGNIZE YOUR SIGNIFICANCE

Week Forty-Six

Keep *Short* Accounts

What I mean by keeping short accounts is to forgive quickly or ask for forgiveness as soon as you realize you have wronged someone. For example, during the 1990s I had a townhouse listed for sale for a couple who was moving out of state. I received a call from a woman inquiring if they would be willing to lease it. I promised to contact the seller to see if leasing was an option for them but I forgot to do it. A week or so later I received a call from this seller who was obviously upset and was demanding a meeting immediately. I later learned this woman had bumped into my seller outside their townhouse and told them of our conversation. After a rocky meeting covering the marketing, they asked me if I had received a call regarding leasing their unit. Then I remembered the woman who was interested in a lease. My reaction to the sellers was, "I blew it. I did receive a call from someone asking about leasing and I forgot to call you. Please forgive me." Needless to say, they were not expecting me to so quickly and emphatically confess my neglect and to also ask for forgiveness. The listing was saved and I ended up selling it for them instead of leasing it, which was what they ultimately wanted.

When you screw up, quickly ask for forgiveness. When someone treats you wrong, forgive them. However, you should not allow yourself to be a doormat either. Forgive and move on.

Live the Dream

Forgiveness is a gift you give yourself.
Suzanne Somers

Take Inspired Action

Who has wronged you? _____
1. Write them a letter telling them how you feel and that you are making a choice to forgive them.
2. Once written, read the letter out loud to no one but yourself.
2. After reading the letter, begin to tear it into tiny pieces which can never be put back together again. Let that serve as a metaphor for your forgiveness, in that you are never going to empower the hurt any more by harboring unforgiveness.

RECOGNIZE YOUR SIGNIFICANCE

Week Forty-Seven

KEEP *the* CHANGE

Do you ever tell a cashier to "keep the change" as a tip or for services rendered above and beyond the call of duty? Some banks are even "cashing" in on this phrase by encouraging customers to use their ATM cards for payment and the amount will be rounded up to the nearest dollar. The difference between the amount of the item purchased and the higher dollar amount is deposited into your savings account. The former is a way to say thank you while the latter is a step, albeit a small one, toward saving money. The most profitable change to keep is the positive change you have been making as you have read and completed the action steps in this book.

You "keep the change" you have made thus far by having accountabilities in place. Then, if you see yourself starting to slip, your accountability partner can step in and help put you back on track. I have several different accountability partners for different facets of my life. Right now, my business coach, John, helps me stay on track with my real estate business. Greg helps me "keep the change" that I am making in my spiritual walk. Dan helps me with my workout routine. You see, you can have more than one accountability partner for multiple areas of your life.

KEEP THE CHANGE

LIVE THE DREAM

Any transition serious enough to alter your definition of self will require not just small adjustments in your way of living and thinking but a full-on metamorphosis.
MARTHA BECK

TAKE INSPIRED ACTION

1. Make a list of the people whom you trust who could serve as an accountability partner for an area of your life you want to change.
2. Call the first person on your list and tell them what you want to change and ask if they will help keep you on track.
3. Set a time to check in weekly to monitor your progress.

Who could be possible accountability partners?

_____
_____
_____
_____

RECOGNIZE YOUR SIGNIFICANCE

Week Forty-Eight

UNHINGE *the* GATE

I have a photograph from the *Los Angeles Times* hanging in my office that shows a dam with millions of gallons of water behind it. Below the dam, is a parched, dry bed that is full of dead trees, brambles and dirt. To the right is a two lane highway with four vehicles parked whose occupants are undoubtedly looking at the scene. The photographer, Joel Lugavere, caught the moment when the gate on the right side of the dam was unhinged and suddenly thousands and thousands of gallons of water began pouring into the channel below.

Too many times, our lives look like this photograph. The water behind the dam signifies our potential that seems to have been locked up. However, that potential is continually putting pressure on the blockage, i.e. the dam. Someone needs to "unhinge the gate" and let the creativity pour forth that will bring new life to the dead, dry bed just on the other side of the dam. You are the person who can unhinge your gate. Stop wondering what the people on the road of life will think about you and let your creativity pour forth. You "unhinge the gate" by speaking to the thing that is blocking you from realizing your potential. I speak TRINSPIRATION™ phrases all of the time to my specific situations. The results have been dramatic and many will be chronicled in my next book. In the meantime, "Unhinge the Gate" in your life.

LIVE THE DREAM

Truly I tell you, if anyone says to this mountain, 'Go, throw yourself into the sea,' and does not doubt in their heart but believes that what they say will happen, it will be done for them.
JESUS

TAKE INSPIRED ACTION

What words do you need to speak to the dam in your life that has been blocking you from your destiny? Write them here:

_____
_____
_____
_____
_____
_____
_____
_____
_____
_____
_____
_____

Let us know at www.trinspiration.com what happened.

RECOGNIZE YOUR SIGNIFICANCE

WEEK FORTY-NINE

DISCOVER *Your* DESTINY

How does one discover his or her destiny? It starts with believing that you have a destiny. Everyone has been given a measure of faith. We must exercise that faith and believe that our destiny is waiting to be discovered. Next we need to ask questions. Why? Because questions will pull out of us the wisdom to find that destiny that is already resident within us. The quality of your questions will determine the quality of wisdom that you discover. Next, we need to spend time with people of destiny—people who have a sense of purpose and are moving through life with a plan committed to finding their destiny.

When you discover your destiny, you may feel surprised; however, you really shouldn't because that destiny has been resident within you from the time you were born. Here's a hint: part of your destiny will be to help other people discover their destiny. You will find your ultimate fulfillment when you help others find theirs.

Discover Your Destiny

Live the Dream

*For I know the plans that I think toward you....
thoughts of peace and not of evil, to give
you a future and a hope.*
God

Take Inspired Action

1. Write down questions about your destiny that you have never before asked yourself.
2. Analyze your sphere of influence and determine which friends are actively seeking their destiny.
3. Make a list of people who seem to have found their destiny and ask questions about how they discovered their purpose.

What questions have I been avoiding asking myself about my destiny?

_____
_____
_____
_____
_____
_____
_____
_____

What friend could I call to talk about discovering my destiny?

_____

RECOGNIZE YOUR SIGNIFICANCE

Week Fifty

PAY IT FORWARD

A movie of the same title was popular several years ago. Haley Joel Osment played an adolescent trying to find his way while being raised by a single mom. His teacher, played by Kevin Spacey, recognized Haley's gifts and encouraged him in his "Pay It Forward" plan. The way it worked is that instead of paying someone back for the nice thing they had done for you, you had to pay it forward to someone else who couldn't repay you.

Here's the deal…even though you weren't supposed to reciprocate to the person who gave you something or did something nice for you, that person still ended up being compensated. The reason is that there is a universal law called the law of reciprocity. When you give, you receive. That's why we need to be careful what it is that we are giving. As I said earlier, seeds produce after their kind.

LIVE THE DREAM

"Are you saying you'll flunk us if we don't change the world?"

"Well no. But you might just scrape by with a C."
CATHERINE RYAN HYDE & LESLIE DIXON
SCREENWRITERS FOR *Pay It Forward*

TAKE INSPIRED ACTION

1. If you are financially capable, pay your struggling friend's utility bill without letting them know.
2. Instead of giving a homeless person money, take them to the grocery store and buy them food.
3. Make an anonymous donation.

Week Fifty-One

TESTIFY to LOVE

In a courtroom trial, the witness must swear to tell the truth, the whole truth, and nothing but the truth. It is a solemn oath and the person swearing to speak only the truth can be tried for perjury if it is revealed that he is lying. Do you realize how powerful your words are and what significance they carry? Your testimony could convict someone of a crime or clear them of wrongdoing. Life or death can, literally, hang on our words.

Every day you are called to testify about something. It may be as mundane as testifying about your opinion of the weather conditions or it might be as important as what you have done with your company's finances. Whatever you are called to testify about, let it be done in love. Love covers a multitude of sins. Love expects the best. Love believes the best. In short, it is the best.

Live the Dream

...speaking the truth in love.
THE APOSTLE PAUL

Take Inspired Action

1. Determine now to only give accurate information in a tactful and kind way.
2. Make sure your tone of voice is respectful.
3. Let your words be few.

RECOGNIZE YOUR SIGNIFICANCE

Week Fifty-Two

LEAVE *a* LEGACY

Two years ago, I sat in a room with hundreds of people who have been touched, motivated, inspired and encouraged by the wise words of Jim Rohn. Luminaries such as Tony Robbins, Brian Tracy, Dr. Denis Waitley, Stuart Johnson, Les Brown and many others, including my father-in-law, shared how Jim had helped shape their lives. While I have been privileged to hear Jim speak from the platform on several occasions, I also had the opportunity to have him come to my house for Thanksgiving and Christmas dinners numerous times over the last 20 years of his life. Dr. Denis Waitley said it best when he said, "Jim didn't leave a legacy, he lived a legacy," meaning that he impacted so many people that he is living through their accomplishments now.

My daughter Kelly has had her life impacted by someone you've probably never heard of. Malachi Smith, the young son of one of Kelly's high school coaches, passed away October of 2009 at the age of three. He succumbed to the ravages of leukemia. Kelly prayed for "Kai," organized a bone marrow drive that yielded 550 donors, and

LEAVE A LEGACY

helped the Make-A-Wish Foundation plan a weekend at Disneyland for the family that started with a parade at her high school. Kelly is currently studying to be a pediatric oncologist because of the legacy that "Kai" and his parents left behind.

You see, you don't have to speak in front of thousands of people to leave a legacy like Jim Rohn did—although you can. You can just be yourself, as Malachi was, and impact people for good, even if you're only three years old.

Life is a series of decisions. If you decide right now to leave a legacy, begin to write down the kinds of things you want to leave behind. Jim left written words, spoken words, and videos of his speeches that will inspire people for years to come. Kai left precious memories that will inspire 900 high school students to live life to the fullest. It is never too early to decide to leave a legacy because we don't know how long we will have on this earth. Jim Rohn had 79 years. Malachi Smith had three years. So I encourage you to "Recognize your significance" and in doing so YOU WILL "leave a legacy."

LIVE THE DREAM

It is up to us to live up to the legacy that was left for us, and to leave a legacy that is worthy of our children and of future generations.
CHRISTINE GREGOIRE

TAKE INSPIRED ACTION

1. By taking "inspired action" you begin the process of building a body of work that will cause you to "leave a legacy."

RECOGNIZE YOUR SIGNIFICANCE

RECOGNIZE YOUR SIGNIFICANCE

Look for these Upcoming
TRINSPIRATION™
products at www.trinspiration.com.

Books:
Give the Command and
Open the Gift—The Christmas TRINSPIRATION™ Collection

•

Calendar

•

Screensaver

•

Apparel: caps, t-shirts

•

Music CD with TRINSPIRATION™ titles like:
"Take the Shot," "Open the Gift" "Recognize Your Significance"

•

TRINSPIRATION™ Newsletter

•

One minute radio Public Service Announcements

•

TRINSPIRATIONTV.com coming soon

•

TRINSPIRATION™ Video coaching